YOU CHOOSE
BOOKS

Surviving the
LE MANS
24 HOURS RACE

AN INTERACTIVE EXTREME SPORTS ADVENTURE

Blake Hoena

Raintree is an imprint of Capstone Global Library Limited, a company incorporated in
England and Wales having its registered office at 264 Banbury Road, Oxford, OX2 7DY –
Registered company number: 6695582

www.raintree.co.uk
myorders@raintree.co.uk

Edited by Nate LeBoutillier
Designed by Bobbie Nuytten
Picture research by Eric Gohl
Production by Katy LaVigne
Originated by Capstone Global Library Limited
Printed and bound in China

ISBN 978 1 474 74368 6
21 20 19 18 17
10 9 8 7 6 5 4 3 2 1

British Library Cataloguing in Publication Data
A full catalogue record for this book is available from the British Library.

Acknowledgements
We would like to thank th[...]
Goddard Automotive, 42, [...]
Sipa USA, 86, ZUMA Pres[...]
Panoramic, 1, 6, 14, 21, 33, [...]
releon8211, background (t[...]

Every effort has been made [...]
Any omissions will be rect[...]

All the Internet addresses ([...]
However, due to the dynam[...]
sites may have changed or [...]
regret any inconvenience t[...]
be accepted by either the au[...]

CONTENTS

ABOUT YOUR ADVENTURE

YOU have a fascination with speed, and that is why you got into racing cars. But you understand that racing is about more than driving fast. There is a strategy to winning, especially in longer races. Drivers need to know how to pace themselves and when to speed up to pass. They need the support of a hard-working pit crew and must be able to drive bumper to bumper at incredible speeds.

As a driver behind the wheel in the Le Mans 24 Hours Race, you will have a chance to make decisions that could propel you to victory or leave you in the dust.

How will you go about competing? Do you have what it takes to win a race like this?

Turn the page to begin your adventure.

CHAPTER 1

TWENTY-FOUR-HOUR RACE

Your interest in the combination of speed and strategy has drawn you to endurance racing. Endurance races are gruelling, lasting anywhere from 6 to 24 hours with the team that covers the most laps in the allotted time winning. They push drivers, crews and cars to the limit.

The most prestigious of these races is called "The 24 Hours of Le Mans". It is often referred to as the "Grand Prix of Endurance and Efficiency" because it is the oldest active endurance race. It also has one of the longest straights, making it both a lengthy and a speedy race. Racing teams must earn invitations to Le Mans. One way to receive an invite is by winning a racing series.

Turn the page.

You and your team have been competing in the Britcar Endurance Championship. You ended up on the winner's podium twice.

You finished well in several other races and had the best season of your racing career. And that is why you now find yourself in the small city of Le Mans, France.

It is a sunny day as you stroll over to the garages. The area is busy with activity as there are a total of 60 racing teams entered in the race. You nod to other drivers, and spot mechanics darting in and out of garages.

Two familiar faces greet you outside your team's garage. Mark and Cindy are the other drivers on your team. It is too strenuous for one driver to race for 24 hours straight. So you, Mark and Cindy will take turns behind the wheel.

"It's almost race day," Mark says, cheerful.

"I think it's about time to get down to business," you say.

You three drive for your team, but a successful racing team needs more than just drivers.

"Hoyt and Lois are waiting inside," Cindy says.

They sit at a small table on the far side of the garage. Hoyt is your crew chief, and Lois is your lead engineer. You, Cindy and Mark walk over to the table to sit down.

The three of you may be the face of your racing team, but Lois and Hoyt are the backbone. Without them and their crew, you couldn't get your racing car to the starting grid. They make sure your team's car is running properly and meets required specifications for every race.

Turn the page.

Racing cars at Le Mans must meet body-size requirements, engine-size limits and restrictions on the flow of fuel to their engines. These regulations even out the competition. No one team gets an advantage by using a larger engine or having a lighter car. To win, they must rely on their cars' efficiency and design. A team's skill, both in the pits and on the track, will also aid its success.

Different classes of cars use different specifications, and at Le Mans teams can compete in several categories.

Le Mans Grand Touring Endurance (LMGTE) cars are similar to high-end sports cars. They have two doors and room for two seats in front. These cars are designed to be driven legally on roads, and street versions of them are available for sale to the public.

Before the start of the Le Mans race, drivers and crews discuss strategy as they wait by their cars.

These LMGTE cars are quite expensive, though. Among them are Ferrari GTEs and Porsche 911 RSRs. Maximum engine size for LMGTEs is 5,500 cubic centimetres (cc). The bigger the engine, typically the more power it can produce and the faster the car can go. Also, these cars must have a minimum weight of 1, 245 kilograms (2,745 pounds) and a max length of 4.8 metres (15.75 feet).

Turn the page.

Then there are the Le Mans Prototype (LMP) cars. These cars are built specifically for endurance racing. As with the LMGTE classes, LMPs must meet certain requirements. But these cars are further divided into two classes: LMP1 and LMP2.

The LMP1 class is for car manufacturers and engine suppliers. These companies have the resources to design and build some of the top racing cars in the world, and they like to use endurance races to show off their products. LMP1s' max-allowed engine size is 5,500cc. They must weigh at least 855 kilograms (1,885 pounds) and have a max length of 4.6 metres (15.25 feet).

The LMP2 class is for racing car teams that are not connected to a specific car maker or engine supplier. These cars are limited to 5,000cc engines. They have a minimum weight of 900 kilograms (1,985 pounds) and a max length of 4.6 metres (15.25 feet).

Cars in each of these classes can be lots of fun to drive, of course. But you have to make a decision. In which class will you, Mark and Cindy be competing?

To drive an LMGTE car, turn to page 15.
To drive an LMP1 car, turn to page 43.
To drive an LMP2 car, turn to page 71.

CHAPTER 2

LMGTE RACING CAR

The exciting part about racing Le Mans Grand Touring Endurance (LMGTE) cars is that you get to drive some of the coolest sports cars on the road. The versions of these high-end streetcars you'll be racing are modified from their street-legal counterparts for safety reasons.

The LMGTE class is divided into two groups. There is a category for LMGTE-Pro, or professional, racers and one for LMGTE-Am, or amateur, racers. Professionals can earn prize money for doing well, but beginner racers usually compete in the amateur class. Which class do you race in?

To race LMGTE-Pro, turn the page.
To race LMGTE-Am, turn to page 19.

You look back at your team's car. It is sleek with a spoiler on the rear and yellow tinted headlights up front. On the sides and on the front is a green square with a white number 66. The colour tells other drivers that you race in the LMGTE-Pro class.

"Who's going to run qualifying?" Lois asks.

"Let me," you say.

"And me!" Cindy jumps in.

For qualifying, each team nominates two drivers. They have 20 minutes to race a few laps around the course. The average of each driver's best lap determines your team's position on the starting grid.

Qualifying laps are run a couple of days before race day. You go first.

You have already taken a few test runs, so the course is familiar to you, and your car handles well. You clock a best lap of 3:51.429 around the 13.63-kilometre course. With about 10 minutes left, you head into the pits. You hop out of the car so that Cindy can get buckled in. She notches a best lap of 3:52.957, which means your team's average time is just over 3:52. That gives you the 38th best qualifying time out of 60 cars.

The faster LMP racing cars take up the first 33 spots. So at 38th you are sitting towards the front of the LMGTE cars.

A couple of days later, it is time to race. You are at the garage bright and early. Everyone is tense. Mechanics crawl all over the car. Hoyt and Lois shout out instructions. Cindy and Mark pace nearby.

Turn the page.

You get into your racing suit and hop in the car minutes before the start. The pit crew then rolls the car to its spot on the grid.

"Less than a minute to start," Hoyt radios you. "How's the car running?"

It rumbles as you flex your fingers around the steering wheel. "Purring like a tiger," you reply.

Moments later, the countdown starts.

"Five . . . four . . . three . . . two . . . one . . ."

You want to get off to a strong start. What will you do when the starting flag drops?

To accelerate hard to get a speeding start, turn to page 22.

To press slowly on the accelerator for a rolling start, turn to page 24.

You look back at your team's car. It is sleek with a spoiler on the rear and yellow-tinted headlights up front. There is an orange square on the sides and one on the front with a white number 66 in it. The colour tells other drivers that you race in the LMGTE-Am class.

"Who will run qualifying?" Lois asks.

"How about you and Mark?" Cindy suggests, turning to you. "I want to drive the last stint."

"Sounds good," you say.

For qualifying, two drivers from each team have 20 minutes to take a few laps around the course. The average of each driver's best lap determines a team's position on the grid. Mark clocks 3:57:583, and then you put up a mark of 3:56.257. With an average just under 3:57, you are 51st out of 60 cars.

Turn the page.

That is actually not bad.

The faster LMP cars take up the first 33 spots. Next are the LMGTE-Pro drivers. You will be sitting towards the front of the LMGTE-Am cars.

On race day, you get to the garage bright and early. You watch as mechanics crawl all over the car.

You walk over to Cindy and Mark. Mark high-fives you, and Cindy says, "Get off to a strong start!"

Because you had the best qualifying time, it was decided to let you start the race. You put on your racing suit and helmet. When the time comes, you crawl into the car and get strapped in. Minutes later, the crew rolls the car to its spot on the starting grid.

Fans fill the stands at Le Mans to cheer on their favourite cars and drivers.

Engines roar. Crews shout excitedly. A murmur goes up from the tens of thousands of people in the stands. The countdown begins.

"Five . . . four . . . three . . . two . . . one . . ."

What do you do when the starting flag drops?

To accelerate hard to get a speeding start, turn the page.

To press lightly on the accelerator for a rolling start, turn to page 24.

The countdown hits zero, and you step hard on the accelerator. Your engine roars and you tyres screech. Your car leaps forward. You dart between other cars and jump to the front of all the LMGTE cars. It's not even the first lap.

"What are you doing?" Hoyt yells through the radio. "The safety car is still on the track!"

Endurance races use rolling starts instead of standing starts. A safety car leads the racers out of the gates. The racers keep pace with the safety car and must stay in their starting grid positions.

A slow rolling start is done for safety reasons. Cars can sputter and stall if they accelerate too fast, and that could cause an accident with 60 cars all speeding out of the gates.

"The race steward has ordered you to the pits," Hoyt says. "We're being penalised."

"Aw, man!" you say. You thought you were jumping off to a good start. Instead, you broke an important rule.

You drive around the track and then head into the pits. You see Hoyt talking to a race official.

"We're receiving a three-minute stop and go penalty," Hoyt explains.

That means you have to wait in the pits for three minutes before rejoining the race. Meanwhile, the other cars zoom around the track. By the time you get back in the race, you are dead last. Your team is never able to make up for the bad start.

THE END

To follow another path, turn to page 13.
To learn more about the Le Mans 24 Hours Race, turn to page 103.

When the cars in front of you move, you pull away slowly. You try to keep pace, not pass. You remember that at Le Mans – as at most endurance races – a rolling start is used. A safety car leads the racers out of the gate and sets the pace for the first laps. During this time, no cars are to pass each other. Once race officials determine that racing conditions are safe, the safety car pulls off the track. The green flag drops, and the real racing begins.

When you see the green flag, you accelerate. The engine roars. Your car lunges forward.

Le Mans is a 24-hour race, but that doesn't mean it is slow. Its long straight, known as the Mulsanne Straight, is nearly 6.5 kilometres long with two narrow turns called chicanes to slow things down. Cars can speed up to more than 400 kilometres (250 miles) per hour.

You are running fifth in your class. If you can at least get into third, you'll stand on the winner's podium. Pass the four cars in front of you, and you will have won the race of your life.

During the first laps, you get the feel of the course and how your car is handling. You make no risky manoeuvres and simply hold your spot.

After about 45 minutes, Hoyt radios, "You're coming up on lap 12."

That means it's time to refuel. Less than a minute later you zoom out of the pits.

As you are about to hit the straight, white lights flash behind you. In your rear view you see the number 8 on a red background. One of the other cars is on your bumper.

To move over to let the car pass, turn the page.
To fight the car off, turn to page 28.

Your car has yellow headlights. This car has white headlights, meaning it is in the LMP class. It is common practice for slower cars to let faster cars pass. Also, it could be risky trying to hold off a speedy LMP racing car.

When you head into the straight, you let the number 8 car cut under you. It zooms past.

As the race goes on, you pit to stop for fuel every 12 laps. That is one stint.

"We're changing tyres on your fourth stint," Hoyt radios.

That means your next pit stop will take a bit longer.

You have been driving for about three hours now. While you have some of the fast LMP cars roar past you, you have kept on the same lap as the leading LMGTE cars in your class.

It is still early in the race. At Le Mans, racers can be behind the wheel for up to four hours before taking a break. Do you race another stint or do you let Cindy take over at the next pit stop?

To keep driving, turn to page 30.
To change drivers, turn to page 31.

You have fought hard for your position, so you don't want to get passed. As you hit the Tertre Rouge, the turn leading into the straight, the car behind you tries to duck under you. You cut in front of it.

White lights flash again as you accelerate into the straight.

The car behind you drifts to the outside. You do the same. Then you turn sharply into a chicane to cut the car off. But you are going too fast.

As the curve straightens out, you can't keep the car on the track. Dirt and gravel fly everywhere as you spin out.

When you hit a retaining wall, there is a loud *bang*. Your body is shaken by the impact.

"You all right?" Hoyt asks. There's concern in his voice.

You feel rattled, but reply, "Yeah, I'm okay. I guess I hit the wall pretty hard."

"Why didn't you just let number 8 pass?" Lois shouts. "It's not even in our class."

Then it dawns on you. Your car has yellow lights, not white, and a different-coloured number square. The car trying to pass was a much faster LMP car. You should have known that and just let it pass.

Now your race is over.

THE END

To follow another path, turn to page 13.
To learn more about the Le Mans 24 Hours Race,
turn to page 103.

You don't feel tired, so you tell Hoyt you'll do another stint. Hoyt agrees. The pit crew goes to work filling the fuel tank. When that's done, they swap all four tyres. Just over a minute later, you zoom off.

At the next pit stop, Cindy takes over behind the wheel. Again, the car is refuelled, which takes another minute or so before she speeds off.

This strategy proves costly. You had one long pit stop to change tyres. You had another long stop to swap drivers. It would have saved time to change tyres and drivers at the same stop. Over the course of a long race, each second counts.

Because of the extra time spent in the pits, you finish the race near the bottom of your class.

THE END

To follow another path, turn to page 13.
To learn more about the Le Mans 24 Hours Race,
turn to page 103.

Having to change tyres means a lengthy pit stop. It also takes time to change drivers. You decide it is more efficient to do both at the same pit stop. That way all the other pit stops will be shorter, refuelling stops.

Just over a minute later, you watch as your car zooms out of the pits. Cindy is now driving.

Every 12 laps, your car comes in to refuel. Then after the fourth stint, Cindy swaps with Mark. In a few more hours, it will be your turn once again.

The race goes well for your team because of its pit strategy. You are still towards the front of your class. Each stint lasts a bit more than three hours. So after you, Cindy and Mark have each raced one turn, you are less than a quarter of the way through the race.

Turn the page.

You feel rested as you start your next turn at the wheel. Still, driving is exhausting. You have sudden braking as you come upon a corner and then quick acceleration out of a turn. Your body is constantly being jostled around. You grip the steering wheel tightly as you jockey for position while driving bumper-to-bumper with other cars. You are constantly stepping on the brake, accelerating, or using the clutch to shift gears.

While in the car, you hardly have a second to relax a muscle.

So far, your team has held its own. You are running fourth in your class. But just driving well, and having a good strategy, won't win the race. You also need to take risks, and saving time in the pits is key.

You could start running an extra lap between refuelling, going 13 laps instead of 12. Or you could do an extra stint between tyre changes. That would mean swapping drivers and tyres after five refuellings instead of four.

To run an extra lap between refuelling, turn the page.

To run an extra stint between changing tyres, turn to page 36.

"You're coming up on lap 12," Hoyt radios. "Come in to refuel."

"Let me do another lap," you say. "Maybe we can pick up some time."

You zoom by the pit entrance and head into the Dunlop Curves. You gain on the car ahead and then brake, slowing to less than 160 kilometres (100 miles) per hour. This is a tricky part of the course: There's a quick right turn, then a quick left turn before you drive under the Dunlop Bridge.

The radio is quiet until you hit a straight.

"The third place car pitted," Hoyt says, "so you jumped ahead of it."

"Yes!," you shout back. That'll put you on the winner's podium.

"Don't get excited," Lois cuts in. "You're driving on fumes."

Sports cars usually don't get a lot of distance out of a litre of gas. The faster a car races, the less efficiently its engine runs, so the more fuel it burns. Also, all the accelerating during a race burns fuel quicker. Lois would have calculated precisely how many laps the car could go before needing to be refuelled.

You slow down to take the sharp Muslanne turn at the end of the straight. When you try to accelerate, the car sputters. You are still kilometres from the pits when it rolls to a stop. You hear the roar of other cars whipping by you.

Your risk did not pay off. You are out of fuel, and your race is over.

THE END

To follow another path, turn to page 13.
To learn more about the Le Mans 24 Hours Race,
turn to page 103.

Driving on worn tyres is tricky. The more wear there is, the worse a tyre grips the road. That not only affects the car's handling, but worn tyres slow a car down.

But you feel it is less of a risk than to push off refuelling. You ask Hoyt to let you do another stint on the tyres. Hoyt agrees.

"That could buy us some time," Lois adds.

After just a short refuelling pit stop, you head back onto the course.

You head into the Dunlop Curves and drive under the Dunlop Bridge, which looks like a large tyre arching over the racetrack. Then you are through the Esses, a pair of sharp turns, before you're into the straight and accelerating. Soon your car is zooming along in excess of 320 kilometres (200 miles) per hour.

Pit crews play an important role in
determining the winners at Le Mans.

"How's it handling?" Hoyt asks over the radio.

Around the Esses, you felt your car slip a bit.
You couldn't take the turns as tightly as
you wanted.

"A bit loose," you say, "but I'm all right."

"Good," Hoyt says. "Because we beat the 75
car out of the pits."

Turn the page.

"Yes!" you say. That puts you into third place.

After a few laps, however, your excitement wears down. You can tell you're running a little slower, and you need to drive more carefully around the turns so as not to slide off the track.

"The number 75 car is creeping up on you," Hoyt says.

You have a car trying to pass you and take third place from you. How do you drive?

To drive defensively to keep from being passed, go on to the next page.

To drive offensively to try to pull away, turn to page 40.

You fought hard to get to third place. You don't want to lose it, so you try to keep the car from passing. As it cuts inside on a turn, you dart down to block it. Then out of the turn, the car goes to the outside. You jerk the wheel over to stay in front of it. But you feel your car slip. Your worn tyres don't have great traction, and you slide off the track. You hit the grass and spin out.

By the time you get your car back on the track, it is too late. You've dropped another place. You are unable to catch up to the cars in front of you and finish the race in the middle of the pack in your class.

THE END

To follow another path, turn to page 13.
To learn more about the Le Mans 24 Hours Race,
turn to page 103.

With your worn tyres, you don't want to make any risky moves. You just drive as fast as you can until the end of your last stint.

Only, that isn't fast enough. Around one of the turns, the number 75 creeps up on the outside. It is quicker to accelerate into the straight and passes you.

But in the end, that is okay. Next time you pit, you swap places with Cindy. New tyres are also put on the car. Then she zooms off.

With fresh tyres, she's now faster than the LMGTEs in front of her. She catches up to the 75 car and passes it after a few laps.

It's coming down to the wire. And because you decided to do the extra stint on the tyres, Cindy will not need to change them again before the end of the race. But the third place car does.

Cindy makes a quick pit stop to refuel, but the other team also needs to change tyres and refuel. The need for their lengthy pit stop allows Cindy to get out of the pits quicker and retake third place.

You turn to Mark and high-five him. All around you, the pit crew celebrates.

Cindy has to race hard to hold off the 75 car, but when the chequered flag is waved and she crosses the finish line, third place is yours. You and Mark join Cindy up on the winner's podium to celebrate your solid finish.

THE END

To follow another path, turn to page 13.
To learn more about the Le Mans 24 Hours Race, turn to page 103.

CHAPTER 3

LMP1 RACING CAR

The fastest cars competing at the 24 Hours of Le Mans are Le Mans Prototypes (LMPs). They can top 320 kilometres (200 miles) per hour and are the fastest closed-wheeled cars on the track.

You feel honoured to have been asked to race for a company that sponsors an LMP1 racing car team. It means that your skills on the track have been noticed. Only the best of the best get to compete at this level.

You peek back to look at your car. It's a gorgeous piece of machinery. Simply put, it looks fast. It has a low, aerodynamic profile. If you stood next to it, the top of its enclosed cockpit would come up to about your waist.

Turn the page.

There are a few sponsor decals. But on the sides and front there is a white number 8 on a red square – the colour tells other drivers that you race in the LMP1 class. Your car also has white headlights to distinguish it from cars in the LMGTE class.

LMP racing cars can have different types of engines. Petrol engines are usually bigger, while hybrid engines have an electric motor to help them run more efficiently. Which type of engine would you like to race with?

To race with a hybrid engine, go on to the next page.
To race a with a petrol-fuelled engine, turn to page 49.

Although Le Mans has always been a race about speed, reliability and efficiency also matter. So, it is a perfect race for carmakers to test new technologies, such as hybrid cars.

Most hybrid cars use batteries to supply their electric motor with power. But the weight from hefty batteries can slow racing cars down. So LMP1 hybrids (LMP1-H) often use a flywheel connected to the car's braking system. When the car brakes, the flywheel collects the energy from the car's momentum. This energy is then transferred to an electric motor that powers the car's front wheels.

Starting in 2012, hybrid cars have been dominating Le Mans. An Audi R18 e-tron Quattro took the chequered flag that year and again in 2013 and 2014. In 2015 and 2016, a Porsche 919 hybrid won.

Turn the page.

With a hybrid car, your team has a solid chance of doing well.

"Let's get down to business," Hoyt grunts.

There are numerous things to go over and discuss. You talk about driving rotations, pit strategies and what to do if any mechanical problems occur.

"Since Mark and Cindy are the more experienced drivers, they will run qualifying," Lois says.

They clock an average time of 3:27:683, which is the eighth best time out of 60. You'll start near the front, but towards the back of the pack of nine LMP1 cars. Your work will be cut out for you.

The next couple of days are a whirlwind. Mechanics constantly check the car.

Lois goes over her notes with you, Mark and Cindy. Hoyt grunts out orders.

Next thing you know, it is race day. Mark is strapped into the driver's seat, and the crew rolls your car out to the starting grid.

You watch the starting flag drop. Engines roar and cars whip around the track.

Turn the page.

Mark drives 14 laps and then pits to refuel, which is one stint. On the fourth stint, Cindy gets behind the wheel. The car is refuelled, and Hoyt has the tyres changed.

Cindy follows the same schedule. On her fourth stint, she gets out so that you can strap yourself in.

You drive 14 laps and then pit. Being efficient at pit stops is crucial to winning long races. Any lost seconds in the pit affect the outcome of a race, but safety is also a concern with cars speeding in and out of the pits.

Do you leave the car running during your pit stop, so that you can get off to a faster start, or do you turn the engine off?

To leave the engine running, turn to page 52.
To turn the engine off, turn to page 53.

Back in 1996, Joest Racing team used an LMP Porsche WSC-96 to win Le Mans. Since then, almost every winning car at Le Mans has been a petrol-powered LMP. They are not as fuel-efficient as hybrid cars, but you like their bigger, more powerful engines.

"Let's get ready to go to work here, okay, team?" Lois says. "Mark and Cindy are going to run qualifying."

You are the newest member of the team, so that doesn't come as a surprise to you.

A couple of days before the race starts, your team runs qualifying. Mark and Cindy clock an average time of 3:22:327. That is fourth best. You will start near the front of the 60 cars entered in the race, but in the middle of the nine LMP1 cars.

Turn the page.

The race starts a couple of days later. The garage is a madhouse. Mechanics do final checks. Hoyt shouts out orders, and Lois constantly goes over her notes with you.

Mark gets strapped into the driver's seat. The crew rolls your car out to the starting grid.

You watch the starting flag drop. Engines roar, and cars whip around the track.

Mark drives 13 laps and then pits to refuel, which is one stint. Then on the fourth stint, Cindy takes over behind the wheel. The car is refuelled, and the tyres are changed.

Cindy follows the same schedule. She pits every 13 laps to refuel. On the fourth stint, she gets out of the car, and you take her place. The pit crew refuels the car, and then the tyres get changed.

The fastest modern pit crews can
refuel a car in less than a minute.

Once you are given the green light, you hit
the accelerator.

You turn left, out of the pit lane into the
middle, accelerating, lane. You see a slower
LMGTE class car in the far left fast lane just
ahead of you. Do you speed up to pass or do you
move into the lane behind the slower car?

To pass the LMGTE car on the right, turn to page 55.

To get behind the LMGTE car, turn to page 56.

You don't want your car stalling and losing time, so you keep the engine running. As a crew member hooks up the fuel line, a race steward walks up to Hoyt.

Hoyt's voice comes over the radio. "You forgot to kill the engine. So we're being given a penalty."

The crew member unhooks the fuel line. Then everyone steps back from the car. No work can be done during the penalty. You turn off the engine, and precious seconds tick away.

When the penalty is over, your car is refuelled. You're off again. But every second counts. Penalties make it difficult for your team to catch the race leaders. Try as you might, your team finishes far from the winner's podium.

THE END

To follow another path, turn to page 13.
To learn more about the Le Mans 24 Hours Race, turn to page 103.

Having to restart will take extra time. But it is one of many safety rules for pit stops. Racing officials do not want to risk any accidents during refuelling.

There is even one crew member with a hose to suck up fumes from the fuel, while another is armed with a fire extinguisher in case a problem arises.

Once the car is ready, you zoom out of the pits. Shortly after you get back on the racetrack, you drive under one of the famous Dunlop bridges. It looks like a giant tyre arching over the race.

Next, you will hit the Esses. The course turns right, and then there's a sharp left, which is followed by another right turn.

Turn the page.

Taking the best line on turns will help you catch up to the leaders. Going on the outside of the turn, you can maintain greater speed, but cutting inside is a shorter route through the Esses turns. How do you take the turns?

To go to the outside, turn to page 58.
To cut to the inside, turn to page 60.

You hit the accelerator to get in front of the slower car. As your lane ends, you dart in front of the car on your left. It brakes to avoid hitting you.

"What are you doing?" Hoyt yells over the radio. "You can't pass in the fast lane. That'll cost us."

It does. You are given a 10-second stop-and-go penalty. The next time you pit, a race steward is there. No pit work can be done during the penalty.

Even in a long race like Le Mans, every second counts. What's worse, the rough start to your stint throws you off. You take curves too wide and don't accelerate quickly enough out of turns. Soon one of the other LMP1 cars roars past on the straight.

After your stint, your team is never able to get back into contention.

THE END
To follow another path, turn to page 13.
To learn more about the Le Mans 24 Hours Race, turn to page 103.

You dart behind the slower car. Since it is ahead of you and in the fast lane, it has the right of way, and you don't want to receive a penalty for a pit stop infraction. But as soon as you are back on the track, you flash your lights. Through the rearview mirror, the driver will see the red number square and know you drive the faster car.

Coming into the next turn, you duck down to pass, and the LMGTE does not get in your way. It is standard for slower LMGTE cars to let the speedier LMP cars pass.

Soon, you are on the Mulsanne Straight and accelerating. Your speedometer creeps above 320 kilometres (200 miles) per hour before you have to slow down for a chicane. Then you are speeding away again.

Your time behind the wheel goes well. Only, when you are about to pit, Lois radios you, "The hybrid cars are pitting 14 laps and we are every 13 laps."

Over the course of the race, a team needing to pit fewer times will have a big advantage. What do you do?

To start pitting every 14 laps, turn to page 62.
To keep pitting every 13 laps, turn to page 64.

As you head into the Esses, you take the outside corner. That lets you keep up your speed. You make the first turn, swerve across the lane, and swing wide around the left turn. You've hardly braked.

You swerve across the lane and swing wide around the last turn. But at your current speed, the last right turn is too sharp. Your car slides off the track, and you spin out in the gravel. Luckily, you don't hit the wall.

"You okay?" Hoyt shouts over the radio.

"Yeah," you reply. "I'm fine."

"Then get back on the track!" he shouts.

You whip the car around and slowly get back on the track. You aren't sure how many cars have passed you.

An odd pull coming from the right front tyre makes your stomach drop. You will need to pit to get it looked at. All the time lost means you dropped down in the standings.

While your team finishes the race, the winner's podium remains a faraway fantasy.

THE END

To follow another path, turn to page 13.
To learn more about the Le Mans 24 Hours Race, turn to page 103.

Hitting turns wide might mean you can maintain speed through them. But with S turns, the best way to hit them is by cutting the inside corners. By keeping your line tight, you are not swerving all over the track.

Once through the Esses, you round the Tertre Rouge and hit the straight. You're now creeping up on the fourth place car.

You hit the sharp turn at the end of the straight and cut to the inside. This forces the other car to take a wide turn. You round the corner first and accelerate to grab fourth place.

"Nice driving!" Hoyt shouts over the radio.

The next time around, you head into the pits. Your turn is over, and you'll have about six hours before you get behind the wheel again. You go and eat, drink some water and try to take a nap.

It is dark out the next time you get behind the wheel. As you head out of the pits, the world is a narrow tunnel of light. Your headlights illuminate only what's directly in front of you. Luckily, you've memorized every twist and turn of the course.

After a few laps, Hoyt comes in over the radio. "You're coming up on the 66 car," he says.

As you slow into the Arnage, a sharp 90-degree turn, you see the other car ahead. You can tell it's in the LMGTE-Am class because the square is on an orange background.

You flash your lights as you hit a short straight. Then you are into the Porsche Curves, which end in a short U-turn before taking a sharp right. How do you pass the slower car?

To pass around the outside, turn to page 66.
To pass on the inside, turn to page 68.

"Let me stretch my stints out a lap," you say.

So on the 13th lap, instead of hitting the pits, you continue through the Dunlop Curves before driving under the famous Dunlop Bridge.

Lois comes in on the radio. "I'm not sure about this," she says. "By my calculation, we can run 13.6 laps at best."

But it's too late to turn back now. You have about 10 kilometres to go before your next chance to pit. You speed down the straight, then take the sharp Mulsanne turn. You are about to hit the wicked Indianapolis curve, a 90-degree turn, when you feel the engine sputter. You pull over onto the gravel as your engine dies.

"What's wrong?" Hoyt says.

"Out of petrol," you reply.

To win, you need to take risks. But this one did not pay off. You do not even finish the race.

THE END

To follow another path, turn to page 13.
To learn more about the Le Mans 24 Hours Race,
turn to page 103.

Before each race, Lois carefully calculates how many laps your car can get out of a tank of petrol. So you doubt you could get another lap out of your car and don't want to risk running out of petrol.

"Let's stay the course," you say.

While on the track, you feel the car is handling well. You see one of the LMP1 Hybrid cars creep up on you as you brake into the Indianapolis and then the sharp Arnage turns. But as you accelerate onto the straight, it falls back. Zooming around the Porsche curves, you lose sight of the other car.

But fuel efficiency is your team's downfall. The hybrid cars spend less time in pits and more time on the course. They are putting on more laps, and your team just can't catch up to them.

Your team finishes fourth, so there will be no winner's podium. The podium is dominated by hybrid cars made by the likes of Porsche, Audi Sport Joest and Toyota Racing.

Still, your team has raced well. Once the final lap is run, you, Mark and Cindy are high-fiving the members of your pit crew. It is an incredible feat just to finish the 24 Hours of Le Mans.

THE END

To follow another path, turn to page 13.
To learn more about the Le Mans 24 Hours Race,
turn to page 103.

As the LMGTE car heads into the turn, you take the outside lane around it. In the dark, it is a risky move. You whip around the U-turn, easily nudging ahead of the slower car.

But it is hard to see when the left turn is coming up in the dark. So you take it a little wide and feel something knock the back of your car.

The next thing you know, your car is spinning uncontrollably. Then BAM! You hit the wall. For a second, your world goes black. It takes a moment for you to realise where you are and what happened.

"You okay?" Hoyt says over the radio. "Come on, talk to me."

"Yeah," you mumble. "But the car's not."

Through the windscreen, you see a mangled mess that used to be the front end of your car.

While your race is over, you are able to walk away virtually unscathed. Your car was designed so that in an accident, the cockpit would act like a shell to protect you while the outer parts of the car would break away. Your car will never get back on the track, but you know you will be racing again soon.

THE END

To follow another path, turn to page 13.
To learn more about the Le Mans 24 Hours Race,
turn to page 103.

As the LMGTE car heads into the turn, you duck underneath. The other driver moves over to give you room to pass. There's a quick left turn, and then a straight. As you speed into the straight, you see the other car fall behind in your rearview mirror.

"Nice driving!" you hear Hoyt shout into your radio.

You continue driving well, and by the time your turn is over, your team is in third place.

Then Mark takes over. He is the best driver on your team. He is able to move you up into second place by the time his turn is done.

Then Cindy takes over for the last stretch. While she is unable to catch up to the leader, she is able to hold on to second place. You are cheering her on as the chequered flag drops.

In the sweet celebration, you find yourself on the winner's podium.

Mark and Cindy high-five you as all three of you walk up to the winner's podium. You have just placed in one of the greatest races. It is the highlight of your racing career.

THE END

To follow another path, turn to page 13.
To learn more about the Le Mans 24 Hours Race, turn to page 103.

CHAPTER 4

LMP2 RACING CAR

LMP cars were first introduced to Le Mans back in 1992. In the years leading up to that, only teams that could afford powerful C-class racing cars competed at Le Mans. But race officials wanted more competition to keep the race exciting. So that year, Le Mans Prototype (LMP) and Grand Touring Endurance (LMGTE) categories were introduced. LMP cars have come to dominate Le Mans as they are built specifically for endurance racing.

There are several classes of LMPs. You started off in the LMP3 class, which is for less experienced drivers. Since you have done well, you moved up to the LMP2 class.

Turn the page.

LMP2s are slightly more powerful and faster than LMP3s, just as LMP1s have slightly bigger engines and are faster than LMP2s.

"Let's get this show on the road," Hoyt grunts. "I've got to get the car ready for qualifying."

Your team spends the morning planning its racing strategy, and there's a lot to go over. You talk about the conditions you might face, from driving in the rain to driving at night, and you also determine the driving rotation.

You, Cindy and Mark will each drive a set number of laps and then swap places during a scheduled pit stop. Whoever starts the race will not be driving at the finish. Do you drive at the start or finish of the race?

To drive at the start of the race, go on to the next page.
To drive at the finish of the race, turn to page 75.

You feel that getting off to a strong start is easier than playing catch, so you say, "Let me start."

"Okay, then you and Cindy will drive qualifying," Lois says. "Mark will drive third."

Your team clocks an average lap qualifying time just under 3:37 for the 13.6-kilometre (8.47-mile) course. That puts you at 12th on the starting grid. The faster LMP1 race cars take up the first nine spots. So you will sit towards the front of the 24 LMP2 cars.

On race day, the garage is chaotic. Mechanics perform last-minute checks. Hoyt and Lois run around and shout out instructions.

You get into your racing suit and hop in the car minutes before the start. The pit crew then rolls the car to its spot on the starting grid.

Turn the page.

Minutes later, the countdown begins.

"Five . . . four . . . three . . . two . . . one . . ."

You are off zooming around the track.

During the first few laps, you get a nice feel for how the car will be handling. As you begin the 13th lap, Hoyt radios you, "Come on in to refuel."

The less time spent in the pits, the more time you are on the track. But the pits are also a dangerous place with cars racing in and out.

When you enter the pits, do you zoom in at 80 kilometres (50 miles) per hour – your car has very sharp breaks. Or do you coast in at 56 kilometres (35 miles) per hour?

To speed in, turn to page 77.
To coast in, turn to page 79.

You like the excitement of chasing the chequered flag, so you ask, "Can I drive the last turn?"

Lois looks to Mark and Cindy. "Is that okay with you two?"

They both nod.

"Okay," Lois says. "Then I suppose you and Cindy drive qualifying."

You and Cindy combine for a qualifying time of 3:41. That is the 23rd best out of 60 cars. The faster LMP1 race cars take up the first nine spots, which means your team will be sitting in the middle of the LMP2 cars.

On race day, you watch as Cindy gets buckled into the car. Then the crew rolls it out to the starting grid.

Turn the page.

After 13 laps, Cindy drives into the pits to refuel. Each time she does is one stint. After four stints, she hops out of the car so that Mark can take over. When Mark's turn is done, you hop in the car.

Before your first pit stop, it starts to rain. As you pull in, Hoyt asks over the radio, "Do you want to swap tyres?"

You have only driven one stint on these tyres, and changing tyres adds a lot of extra time to a pit stop. You will fall farther behind the leaders. But right now you are driving on slicks, or smooth tyres.

To change tyres, turn to page 81.
To keep the slicks on, turn to page 85.

You zip into the pit lane, screeching to a halt in front of your garage. Before the crew member can hook up the fuel line, a race steward walks up to Hoyt. He throws his hands up in the air. Then he says over the radio, "You came into the pits too fast. We're receiving a penalty."

During the penalty, no work can be done on the car. Precious seconds tick away.

Turn the page.

Refuelling cars and changing tyres is an essential skill for the best pit crews.

To the race officials, safety is more important than speed, so a speed limit is set in the pits. You were almost 24 kilometres (15 miles) over the set limit.

Your mistake throws off your crew. They take a little longer than normal with the pit stop. By the time you are back on the track, you have dropped a couple of places.

While your team is able to finish the race, mistakes cost you. Lost seconds quickly add up to minutes. You are unable to catch the lead cars in your class. You finish 31st, towards the back of the LMP2 class.

THE END

To follow another path, turn to page 13.
To learn more about the Le Mans 24 Hours Race,
turn to page 103.

More important than speed is safety in the pit stop. The pits are dangerous, with cars zooming in and out, highly flammable fuel and crew members darting around. Racing officials have set a speed limit on entering and exiting the pits. At 56 kilometres (35 miles) per hour, you are just under that limit.

You stop and turn your engine off – another safety rule. Your pit crew refuels the car.

Soon you are off and racing again. Every 13 laps, you come in to refuel. That is one stint. Then on the fourth stint, you get out of the car so that Cindy can get behind the wheel. You have finished racing for a few hours. So you go and get some food and water.

After Mark's turn, you are strapping yourself in again.

Turn the page.

Things have been running like clockwork for your team, and you have slowly moved up in the standings. The race is now more than a third over as each of your stints took a little over three hours. If your team keeps racing well, you could end up on the winner's podium.

On one lap, you catch up to the LMP2 car in front of you. You are heading into Porsche Curves, a series of several back and forth turns, before hitting another short straight.

When do you pass the car in front of you?

To pass on the curves, turn to page 90.
To wait for the straight, turn to page 95.

Slicks are smooth tyres great for gripping dry road. But if any water gets between them and the track, you could slide all over the track. That would be a big problem.

Changing tyres will add time in the pits, but it is a good idea.

"Put on rain tyres," you say. "It's getting wet out there."

"Okay," Hoyt says.

Rain tyres have special treads, or grooves, that help to stop water from getting between the tyres and the road. This allows for much better traction on a wet surface.

Turn the page.

You then zoom out of the pits.

At first you worry that changing the tyres costs you too much time. But as it keeps raining, more and more cars go in to have rain tyres put on. That gives you a chance to move up in the standings.

When you come in to pit at the end of the fourth stint, you hear something over your radio.

Lois says into your ear, "I'm gonna ask you to drive one more stint."

Since you already changed tyres early in your turn, the ones on your car are still all right.

"No problem," you say. Then after refuelling, you are zooming out of the pits.

After your fifth stint, you swap places with Cindy. Before you head off to eat and rest, Lois sits you down.

"With you driving a longer turn, my schedule is thrown off," she says. "We could keep everyone on four stint rotations, but then your last turn would be shorter. Or maybe we could ask Mark and Cindy to drive five stint turns."

Turn the page.

Any time spent in the pits is lost time, so you like the idea of giving Mark and Cindy longer turns. That means you will cut down on one driver change, which can take up precious seconds. But to do so, both Mark and Cindy will have to go an extra stint on worn tyres, which could slow them down. Which plan do you go with?

To ask Mark and Cindy to do longer turns, turn to page 87.

To end the race on a half turn, turn to page 89.

You have fresh tyres on and do not want to spend the extra time in the pits.

"Let's keep running on the slicks," you say.

After refuelling, you are off.

The more surface a tyre has with the road, the more traction it has. Smooth slicks are great for driving on dry tracks. But when water gets between them and the track, a slippery and dangerous situation ensues.

You head into the Indianapolis, a 90-degree turn, and barely avoid sliding off the track. Next is the Arnage, another 90-degree turn. You nearly spin out.

"How's it going?" Hoyt radios.

"I'm sliding all over," you say.

"Better pit and get those tyres changed."

Turn the page.

Before the pits, there's a very tight set of turns
called the Ford Chicanes. To stay on the track,
you creep along, losing valuable time. In the end,
waiting to change tyres costs you. You drop a few
places, and your team can never quite catch up to
the leaders in your class.

THE END

To follow another path, turn to page 13.
To learn more about the Le Mans 24 Hours Race,
turn to page 103.

"Can we ask Cindy and Mark to take longer turns?" you ask.

"Yes, but then you'd end on a four-stint turn," Lois says.

The plan pays off. Mark and Cindy put in five stints each. Their last stints are on worn tyres, so their lap times are a little slower. But in the long run, you end up skipping one lengthy pit stop where you make a tyre and driver change. That saves you more time than you lose with the slower lap times.

Then, with less than four hours left in the race, you are behind the wheel. You zip out of the pits on fresh tyres.

"How's the car feeling?" Hoyt asks.

"Running smooth," you say, as you head into the Dunlop Curves.

Turn the page.

Then you are through the Esses and onto the Muslanne Straight. You get your car going over 320 kilometres (200 miles) per hour.

You are currently running third and on the same lap with the leaders. Luckily for you, the car in second has to make one last pit, so you move up a spot.

You catch up to the leader, the number 47 car, on the Indianapolis. Then it darts ahead, but you are back on its tail as it corners around the Arnage. Your car seems to be running a little faster and handling better – maybe because you have fresher tyres.

You just need to pick the right moment to overtake the car.

To pass going into a turn, turn to page 92.
To pass on the straight, turn to page 93.

"Let's stay the course," you tell Lois. "It would slow us down to race on worn tyres."

"Okay," Lois says.

Your team continues to race well. You slowly creep up in the standings. Then with only a couple of hours left in the race, your team has to pit. At this point in the race, the cars in front have already made their last pit stops. So a long stop to swap drivers and tyres puts you farther behind them.

You zoom out of the pits. But you never have a chance to catch up to the lead cars. When you zoom past the chequered flag you are several laps down.

THE END

To follow another path, turn to page 13.
To learn more about the Le Mans 24 Hours Race,
turn to page 103.

You have several cars to catch before you are among your class leaders, so you want to get ahead of this car as soon as you can. You duck low into the first right turn, but the car moves to block you. So you quickly swing wide into the next, looping left turn. You nose forward, enough so that the car can't move to block you when you hit the right turn.

Next is a quick left turn. As you make it, you feel a hard rap on the back of your car. You look in the mirror to see a car whirling around behind you. You also feel a drag coming from the back, right side of your car.

"What happened?" Hoyt radios you.

"I got clipped," you say. "And something is definitely wrong."

"Head in," Hoyt says.

Luckily, you aren't too far from the pits. You are driving slower, but able to make it in. Once the car is stopped, your crew spins it around and wheels it into the garage.

"Back fender is trashed and rubbing on the tyre," Hoyt says. "We'll get it fixed and change the tyres."

While your team is able to get the car back on the track, you lost a lot of time. You are not able to catch up to the leaders in your class.

THE END

To follow another path, turn to page 13.
To learn more about the Le Mans 24 Hours Race,
turn to page 103.

Your car is handling better, so you decide to overtake the other car on the next turn, the Tertre Rouge. You follow closely, drafting, and build up speed. Before the 45 car hits the turn, you cut under.

You edge forward on the inside corner. You edge ahead around the turn. But by taking the turn as sharply as you had to, you also need to brake a lot.

The 45 car is forced to take the turn wider, but that allows it to keep its speed. When 45 accelerates into the straight, the car overtakes you.

When the chequered flag falls on the lead car, you are still in second place. You hear whoops and yells from the crew over the radio. You may not have won, but second place in your class is a great finish at Le Mans.

THE END

To follow another path, turn to page 13.
To learn more about the Le Mans 24 Hours Race, turn to page 103.

The easiest place to pass a slower car is on a straight. And since you are this close to the finish, you don't want to risk passing on a turn.

You slip behind the 45 car, drafting as it goes around the Tertre Rouge. Then you swing wide, letting your car's momentum shoot you into first place.

Turn the page.

You are well ahead of 45 when you hit the first of the two chicanes on the straight. Then you are around the Muslanne Curve, and you lose sight of the 45 car.

When the chequered flag drops, you are first in your class.

"Woo-hoo!" you shout into the radio. Your crew hoots and yells back.

Afterwards, you walk to the top of the winner's podium with Mark and Cindy. You grab their hands and raise them up in the air.

THE END

To follow another path, turn to page 13.
To learn more about the Le Mans 24 Hours Race,
turn to page 103.

The Porsche Curves are one of the trickiest sections of Le Mans. They start with a nearly 90-degree right turn, and end with a big S curve.

There is still plenty of race left. You don't risk passing anyone through this treacherous stretch.

You race bumper to bumper with the car in front of you. You hope the driver will feel the pressure and make a mistake.

That happens heading into the last turn. The other car ducks down too far into the turn and has to brake hard. You swing outside and pass as you accelerate into the straight.

Cheers come from your radio as your crew gets excited about that move.

On your fourth stint, you pit and unstrap yourself from your safety harness.

Turn the page.

It's Cindy's turn to get behind the wheel. About a minute and a half later, she zooms out of the pits.

After Cindy's turn, Mark gets behind the wheel. Then roughly six hours later, you are driving again.

A few laps into your turn, Hoyt radios, "Accident on the Ford Chicanes."

Then you see the yellow caution flag. You are many kilometres from the accident, but all of the cars around you begin to slow down. Do you pass them, or do you slow down too?

To pass, go on to the next page.
To slow down, turn to page 98.

You have time to pass a few cars before reaching the accident, so you accelerate.

Shortly after passing a car, Hoyt shouts over the radio, "You can't pass during a caution flag! We've been given a drive-through penalty."

On your lap, you have to drive into the pits. You can't stop to refuel. You just drive through at the slow speed set for the pits. This allows other cars to get ahead. You fall back several places.

Your team is still able to finish the race, but because of mistakes like the caution flag violation, your team is never able to catch up to the leaders. Hopefully you've learned something.

THE END

To follow another path, turn to page 13.
To learn more about the Le Mans 24 Hours Race,
turn to page 103.

During a caution flag, no passing is allowed, for safety reasons. Any debris on the track could lead to further accidents.

A safety car sets the pace. With cars having to slow down, they are bunching up into a pack, allowing you to get closer to the cars ahead of you.

It is a little early for your next scheduled pit stop. But with the slow pace, you could pit, refuel and not lose too much ground on the leaders. Or you can stay with the pack and hope to pass the leaders once the caution flag is lifted.

To pit, go on to the next page.
To stay with the pack, turn to page 101.

This is a great time to take an unscheduled pit stop. The other cars are forced to a slower speed, so you do not fall far behind while in the pits. You head in to refuel. Then when the race is at full speed again, you jump ahead of any cars that didn't pit while under the caution.

So far, you have done everything right. You started the race off strong.

Turn the page.

When you hop out of the car after your final turn behind the wheel, the crew gives you high fives as you walk into the garage.

Then you sit back to watch the race. Your success behind the wheel has helped build your team's confidence. Mark has a great run behind the wheel and moves you into fourth place. When Cindy takes over, she is only seconds behind the third place car. On her last stint, you watch as she moves into third around the Tertre Rouge, and then speeds away into the straights.

When the chequered flag drops, everyone in the garage cheers. You and your team made it to the winner's podium in one of the world's most prestigious races.

THE END

To follow another path, turn to page 13.
To learn more about the Le Mans 24 Hours Race,
turn to page 103.

You don't want to fall farther behind, and since you have plenty of fuel and fresh tyres, you don't pit. As some of the other LMP2 cars pit, you make up ground. But soon the caution flag is lifted, and you have to pit to refuel. Now that cars are whipping around at full speed again, you quickly drop back a few places while in the pits. You end up losing more ground than you made up earlier.

Not taking advantage of the caution flag to pit costs your team. You're now running a little farther behind than before the accident. Because of similar mistakes, you are never in contention to overtake the leaders. Your team finishes the race, but towards the back of the LMP2 cars.

THE END

To follow another path, turn to page 13.
To learn more about the Le Mans 24 Hours Race,
turn to page 103.

CHAPTER 5

LE MANS HISTORY

In the late 1800s, Karl Benz developed the first petrol-powered car. Shortly afterwards, the sport of car racing was born.

Racing quickly grew in popularity, with early races focusing mostly on speed. But in 1923, the Automobile Club de l'Ouest (ACO) developed a new kind of challenge. The 24-Hour Race of Le Mans would focus more on reliability than speed. A long endurance race would put more strain on cars and force car makers to build more dependable vehicles. Since 1923, the race has been run annually, except in 1936 and during World War II.

André Lagache and René Léonard won the first Le Mans in a Chenard & Walcker, a French car. The most successful British driver is Derek Bell. He won five times. Perhaps one of the greatest drivers at Le Mans is Tom Kristensen from Denmark. He won Le Mans six years in a row, from 2000 to 2005, and he has a total of nine wins at Le Mans.

Over the years, German car makers have had the most success at Le Mans. Porsche and Audi combine for more than 30 wins. British car makers Bentley and Jaguar have had a lot of success too. In 1966, an American-built car, a Ford GT 40, won Le Mans for the first time and remains the only American-built car to win the race overall.

The Le Mans course is called Circuit de la Sarthe. Sarthe is the area in France where the city of Le Mans is located. The racetrack goes from Le Mans, to the village of Mulsanne, to Arnage, and then back to Le Mans. Originally, it was nearly 18 kilometres (11 miles) long. But many changes have been made over the years, and now it is 13.6 kilometres (8.47 miles) long. Much of the course is on public streets.

The Le Mans race is about more than simply speed. Endurance and efficiency are also key. It takes determination and skill to win. It continues to be a race that car makers and drivers strive to compete in. Winning at Le Mans is proof that a car is well designed and that a team's drivers and crew are some of the best in the world.

DANGERS of LE MANS

Crashes

Crashes have taken the lives of 22 drivers in the history of Le Mans, dating back to 1925. The worst crash in motorsport history occurred at the 1955 Le Mans. A two-car crash killed 83 spectators and one of the drivers, Pierre Levegh.

The burning wreckage of the crash flew into the grandstand, causing the large number of spectator fatalities. In addition to the deaths, more than 100 other spectators were seriously injured.

As the safety features of cars have improved over the years, the number of crashes at Le Mans has fallen. But there are still crashes today. Most recently, Danish driver Allen Simonsen was killed in a wreck during the 2013 Le Mans.

Night driving

Crisp vision is a driver's most vital sensory ability. At night, the simple ability to see is compromised.

Fatigue

One of the elements that makes Le Mans a unique event is the fact that it's a 24-hour race. But with this test of extreme endurance comes a price: driver fatigue.

Other distractions

Distracted driving can lead to reckless driving, and Le Mans is filled with distractions. Other cars, adoring fans and even modern technology can deter the most skilled driver from keeping total focus.

GLOSSARY

aerodynamic   wind resistant

chicane   short, narrow turn on a race track; chicanes are often used to break up long straights

contention   act of competing for a prize

drafting   driving closely behind another car in order to reduce wind resistance

efficient   working without being wasteful of energy

endurance   ability to go long distances while handling hardships and stress

jockey   change position by a series of movements

manoeuvre   difficult movement that takes planning and skill

pit stop   stop during a race during which a car gets refuelled and tyres can be changed

qualifying laps   timed laps around the track that determine the order in which racing cars are lined up at the beginning of a race

reliable   dependable and trustworthy

restrictions   limitations

rolling start   also called an Indianapolis start; type of start in which cars follow a pace car around the track for the first few laps at the beginning of the race

specifications   list of requirements that needs to be followed when designing something

standing start   type of start in which cars are stationary at the beginning of the race

starting grid   section of the track where cars are lined up at the beginning of a race

traction   friction or gripping power that keeps a moving body from slipping on the surface

OTHER PATHS TO EXPLORE

❖ In this book, the paths follow a driver racing in the 24 Hours of Le Mans race. But there are many other members on a racing team. Imagine that you are part of the pit crew. What job would you do, and how would you help your racing team succeed?

❖ Car makers and engine manufacturers use races like the 24 Hours of Le Mans to test and display their newest designs and advancements in their cars. Imagine you work designing racing cars. What new technologies can you imagine that would help your racing team win a race like Le Mans.

❖ For endurance races, teams' cars must meet certain specifications. But imagine no limits on the cars. They could have the biggest engines they wanted and use any type of vehicle. How would a race using cars like that be different?

FIND OUT MORE

BOOKS

Racing Cars (Top Marques), Rob Colson (Wayland, 2015)

Racing Driver: How to Drive Racing Cars Step by Step, Giles Chapman (Thames & Hudson, 2014)

Racing Supercars, Paul Harrison (Franklin Watts, 2014)

WEBSITE

www.dkfindout.com/uk/transport/history-cars/ racing-cars
Learn about the history of cars on this website.

INDEX